D0977630

Pitiless Parodies
and
Other Outrageous Verse

Frank Jacobs

With a Foreword by
Martin Gardner

Dover Publications, Inc.
New York

Copyright

Copyright © 1994 by Frank Jacobs.
All rights reserved under Pan American and International Copyright Conventions.

Published in Canada by General Publishing Company, Ltd., 30 Lesmill Road, Don Mills, Toronto, Ontario.
Published in the United Kingdom by Constable and Company, Ltd., 3 The Lanchesters, 162–164 Fulham Palace Road, London W6 9ER.

Bibliographical Note

This Dover edition, published in 1994, is a new selection of verses by Frank Jacobs. Most of these verses first appeared in *Mad* magazine. "Fame" first appeared in *Punch*. Other verses first appeared in the books *Mad for Better or Verse, Mad About Sports* and *The Highly Unlikely Celebrity Cookbook*. They are reprinted through the courtesy of the publishers. A new foreword has been specially prepared for this edition by Martin Gardner.

Library of Congress Cataloging-in-Publication Data

Jacobs, Frank.
    Pitiless parodies and other outrageous verse / Frank Jacobs : with a foreword by Martin Gardner.
        p.   cm.
    ISBN 0-486-28126-4 (pbk.)
    1. Humorous poetry, American.   2. Parodies.   I. Title.
PS3560.A2498P58   1994   94-472
811'.54—dc20   CIP

Manufactured in the United States of America
Dover Publications, Inc., 31 East 2nd Street, Mineola, N.Y. 11501

For Nick Meglin

Acknowledgments

Kipling and Kilmer, Service and Poe,
How do I honor the debt that I owe?
Browning and Sandburg, Carroll and Field,
What faint esteem do these parodies yield?
Longfellow, Masefield, Thayer and Hood
(All of the others I'd list, if I could)—
Kings of the couplet, rajahs of rhyme,
Iambic icons, untoppled by time;
But words of acknowledgment must be expressed:
"Without whom I couldn't have . . ."—you know the rest.

Foreword

For reasons none too clear, modern poets—there are exceptions—have abandoned rhyme and rhythm for verse that is indistinguishable from prose broken into lines to make it *look* like verse. Is it because this is so easy to do? Why master the difficult art of writing traditional poetry when so few today read poetry? In the years before radio, television and motion pictures, verse was so widely admired that almost every newspaper here and in England printed a daily poem. Today, who reads modern poetry except critics, professors of literature and other poets?

Something curiously similar has happened in painting, again with notable exceptions. Just as the meaning of a poem has a greater impact when there is that magic coincidence of melody and sense, so classical art was a magic blend of recognizable scenes with pleasing patterns of shapes and colors. It takes little talent to paint a canvas all white, or to cut it into a few rectangles of different colors, or to dribble paint on it. It has been said that Jackson Pollock's finest work was lost forever because it splattered on the floor. Robert Frost once likened free verse to playing tennis without a net. The same is true of art without restraints. It is easy to paint or sculpt without rules. It is easy to write verse without rules.

Vers libre is, in fact, an oxymoron. As Gilbert Chesterton wrote in *Fancies Versus Fads*, calling it a new way of writing is like saying that sleeping in a ditch is a new form of architecture, or that eating raw meat is an innovation in cooking. "Prose is not the freedom of poetry; rather prose is the fragments of poetry." Verse is not improved by turning it into prose, he says elsewhere, any more than singing is improved by making it talking.

The largest class of recent poets who are unashamed of musical patterns are the writers of humorous verse. I have a dark suspicion that the reputations of most of today's netless poets will fade more rapidly than those of writers of light and comic verse. The lines of the comedians may jingle and clank, but at least they arouse immediate pleasure and are easy to understand and memorize. They are to great poetry as good cartoons and skillful caricatures are to great visual art. Even nineteenth-century poets of humor—Thomas Hood, for example—can be relished today when many serious poets of the time, once extravagantly praised by critics, have become flyblown.

There are two kinds of unserious versifiers: the masters of light verse—Dorothy Parker, Phyllis McGinley and Ogden Nash, to name just three Americans—and the writers of truly funny poems. Frank Jacobs is in the second group. Readers of *Mad* know him well for his hundreds of hilarious contributions to that magazine, but outside *Mad* circles the general public has yet to discover his genius. I consider him the funniest writer of comic verse in English. No one, but no one, can parody a familiar poem with greater deftness. Fans of the Mighty Casey will recognize at once the gemlike perfection of the following line from "Casey at the Dice":

> For Casey, lucky Casey, was advancing to the felt!

Writers of light verse arouse smiles. Jacobs generates chuckles and belly laughs.

Emily Dickinson once said that the only way to recognize great poetry is by a tingling of your spine and a feeling that the top of your head blew off. Jacobs' verse, of which we have here a choice selection, may not tingle your spine, but it will tickle your ribs.

And now, relax, start turning the pages, and enjoy the work of a master humorist and craftsman.

MARTIN GARDNER

Contents

Great Poems Updated

Father William

"You are old, Father William," the young man said,
 "And your hair now should be very white;
But it's black and it's bushy all over your head;
 Do you think, at your age, this is right?"

"It's touched up," Father William replied to his son,
 "And with transplants my baldness is ended;
Though I'm now 84, I appear 41,
 And the chicks think I'm groovy and splendid."

"You are old," said the youth, "and I thought I would find
 That your face would be sagging and wrinkling;
But your skin is as smooth as a baby's behind
 And of lines there is scarcely an inkling."

"Had a face-lift," the old man replied, "just last year;
 Cost a bundle, but now I feel human;
I used to come on like Redd Fox or Will Geer,
 But now I'm hot stuff like Paul Newman."

"You are old," said the youth, "for despite your new look,
 You are bogged down in hopeless senility;
With chicks you come off as a helpless old schnook,
 Despite all your claims of virility."

"Shut your face," Father William replied; "though it's true
 That I purchased new glands last September,
Whatever I'd hoped for my body to do,
 My mind is too old to remember."

Kubla Khan

In Xanadu did Kubla Khan
A stately pleasure-dome decree,
With marble bathtubs in each john
And ev'ry room a great salon
To please his family.

A builder came, surveyed the land,
Proposed a deal for them to sign:
"I'll build it in a year as planned;
'Twill cost you only fifty grand."
And Kubla said, "That's fine."

No work was done for half a year,
A fact that Kubla didn't like;
Said he, "You're way behind, I fear;
How come there are no workers here?"
The builder said, "A strike."

Two years, then three went by before
Poor Kubla stood inside his hall;
The den, he noted, lacked a door,
And three rooms on the second floor
Had not been built at all.

"Good God!" he screamed, "You can't deny
That what you've built here is a mess!
I'd like to know the reason why!"
To which the builder did reply,
"Poor workmanship, I guess."

So Kubla Khan left Xanadu,
Disgusted with his pleasure-dome;
And now near Highway twenty-two
He lives as many others do
Inside a mobile home.

The Village Blacksmith

Under a spreading chestnut tree
　　The village smithy stands;
The smith, a wily man is he
　　With itchy, greedy hands,
For he knows he's getting twice the sum
　　His fifth-rate work commands.

A man brings in a limping mare
　　And says with some remorse,
"She's bothered by a nail that's loose";
　　The smith says, "Sure, of course,
But I'm jammed up in the shop just now—
　　You'll have to leave your horse."

Next afternoon the man returns
　　And hears the awful news;
"Your mare dropped dead," the smith explains,
　　"While trying on new shoes,
But I've found you a nice gelding
　　At a price you can't refuse."

The customer pays through the nose
　　As only suckers can;
The clever smith has carried out
　　His calculated plan;
Now tell me, readers, would you buy
　　A used horse from this man?

Abdul A-bul-bul Amir

The sums of the profits from oil-fields are great,
　　Exceeding ten zillion per year,
And the richest of sheiks was the Grand Potentate
　　Called Abdul A-bul-bul Amir.

When they wanted a man for enforcing the ban
  That filled Western nations with fear,
The lesser sheiks went to the split-level tent
  Of Abdul A-bul-bul Amir.

"Our shipments shall stop, and we'll sell not a drop
  Until their reserves disappear;
They'll crawl at our feet, which will be very sweet,"
  Said Abdul A-bul-bul Amir.

"But what of our profits?" the other sheiks asked,
  "They'll soon drop to nothing, we hear."
"It's worth any loss just to prove that we're boss,"
  Said Abdul A-bul-bul Amir.

So, swearing by Allah, they held back their oil,
  Which paralyzed lands far and near
(The Swiss they still sold, for their banks held the gold
  Of Abdul A-bul-bul Amir).

But after a while there was oil leaking out,
  Which seemed to the sheiks rather queer;
"I'm starting to think in our group there's a fink,"
  Said Abdul A-bul-bul Amir.

The trouble, you see, is when Arabs agree,
  Their pledges are seldom sincere;
The cause of that leak was that crafty old sheik
  Called Abdul A-bul-bul Amir.

O Captain! My Captain!

O Captain! My Captain!
Our graft has run its course;
I hear the new Commissioner is shaking up the force;
Just yesterday McSweeney was dismissed for taking bribes;
I fear that you and I are next—I do not like the vibes.

O Captain! My Captain!
We soon will feel the heat;
They nabbed Lieutenant Harrigan, and now he pounds a
    beat;

They've thrown the book at Sergeant Hicks for fencing
   stolen goods,
And Swenson's turning in his badge for shaking down two
   hoods.

O Captain! My Captain!
I fear we are dead ducks;
A Broadway pimp's confessed he slipped us seven hundred
   bucks;
We now must pay the penalty; to trial we'll be brought;
Let's hope we get Judge Patterson—I hear he can be bought.

The Raven

Once upon a midnight dreary, while I pondered, weak and
   weary,
Over many a quaint and curious volume of forgotten lore—
Suddenly I heard a choking, as of someone near to croaking,
And I saw a raven poking 'round the edge of my front door;
"Where've you been?" I asked the raven, as he staggered
   through my door;
        Quoth the raven, "On the shore."

I could see his coat was icky, ev'ry feather gooey, sticky,
From some tanker's oil slick he fell into beyond the shore;
Also, there was no mistaking pesticides he'd been intaking,
Causing him to lie there shaking, while he threw up on my
   floor;
"Are you ill?" I asked the raven, while he threw up on my
   floor.
        Quoth the raven, "At death's door."

As I saw the end was nearing, suddenly I started fearing
Ravens might be disappearing like the dodo bird before;
"Right on, Mac," he said, voice straining, "though I'm really
   not complaining,

I'm the last one who's remaining of those flocks killed by the
     score";
"No," I shrieked, "there must be one surviving those killed
     by the score."
               Croaked the raven, "Nevermore."

Trees

I think that I shall never see
A poem as lovely as a tree;
I'd hoped, of course, that there would be
A tree still left for me to see;
Some lumber firm from out of town
Has chopped the whole darn forest down;
But I'll show up those dirty skunks—
I'll go and write a poem called "Trunks."

My Last Duchess

That's my last duchess painted on the wall—
One eye's been covered by Big Mike's scrawl,
Inscribed in red, AVENGER'S TURF,
With spray-gun supplied by Creepy Murph;
And along her brow, the purple script of Nick's—
KING KONG'S A FAG and FREE THE LAPLAND SIX;
That's my last duchess painted on the wall—
Her chin's decorated with MARGE DIGS PAUL,
And just above, in letters two feet high—
MICKEY ROONEY LIVES and BUTTON YOUR FLY;
I come by and look at her from time to time;
Down the length of her nose run the words EAT SLIME;
That's my last duchess painted on the wall;
Who added her mustache I can't recall;
You'll notice, in orange, THE CRUDS ARE HERE,
Which crosses her face from ear to ear,

And see that purple blob running down her cheek?
If you look real close, it says IZZY THE FREAK;
That's my last duchess—Why should I paint others
To have 'em destroyed by those spray-happy mothers?

The Little Toy Dog

The little toy dog is covered with dust;
The Tinkertoys rot on the shelf;
The little toy soldiers are gathering rust,
And the teddy bear sits by himself.

The little toy engine won't puff any more,
And, golly, I feel like a boob—
I've filled up his playroom with toys from the store,
But my kid won't get up from the tube.

The Passionate Shepherd to His Love

Come live with me and be my love,
As man and wife, 'neath God above;
We're sure to find eternal bliss—
With open marriage we can't miss.

No joys will equal yours and mine,
Partaking of a love divine,
And should we find that life's a bore,
We'll swing with Jane and Bob next door.

Or, maybe, if it's opportune,
We'll move into a sex commune
And mix it up with studs and chicks
In orgies watching porno flicks.

Perhaps you'll dig companionship
With leather gear and boots and whip;
If so, my love, I'll serve you well
And let you chain me in a cell.

So wed me now, my precious thing,
And be my wife and wear my ring;
Yes, let our married days begin
So we won't have to live in sin.

If—

If you can buck a mob of lady shoppers
    And get outside without a scratch or bite;
If you can get a dentist for your choppers
    To fix a toothache on a Sunday night;
If you can smack a truck with your jalopy
    And make the driver think he was to blame;
If you can be a loafer, poor and sloppy,
    Yet have the world think you're some famous name;

If you can change a tire on the thruway,
    While stranded in the busy center lane;
If you can find a foolproof, tried-and-true way
    To housebreak an impossible Great Dane;
If you can find another way to open
    A sardine tin when you have lost the key;
If you can find a fumbled bar of soap in
    Your shower when the suds won't let you see;

If you can rid your house of dull relations
    By faking mumps or plague or Asian flu;
If you can go through tax investigations
    And somehow wind up with them owing you;
If you can read these verses as we list 'em
    And answer "Yes" to each and every one;
Then, Charlie, you have really licked the system—
    And now we wish you'd tell us how it's done.

Celebrities & Such

Hollywood Jabberwocky

'Twas Bogart and the Franchot Tones
Did Greer and Garson in the Wayne;
All Muni were the Lewis Stones,
And Rooneyed with Fontaine.

"Beware the deadly Rathbone, son!
Don't Bellamy the Barrymore!
Beware that you the Greenstreet shun,
And likewise Eric Blore!"

He took his Oakie firm in hand,
Long time the Bracken foe to quell;
He stopped to pray at Turhan Bey,
And murmured, "Joan Blondell."

And as he Breened with Jagger drawn,
The deadly Rathbone, eyes Astaire,
Came Rafting through the Oberon
And Harlowed everywhere!

Sabu! Sabu! And Richard Loo!
The Oakie gave a Hardwicke smack!
He seized its Flynn, and with a Quinn,
He went Karloffing back.

"And didst thou Dunne the Rathbone, Ladd?
Come Grable in the Eddy, boy!
O Alice Faye! O Joel McCrea!"
He Cagneyed in his Loy.

'Twas Bogart and the Franchot Tones
Did Greer and Garson in the Wayne;
All Muni were the Lewis Stones,
And Rooneyed with Fontaine.

The Ballad of Oprah and Phil

The stars that you see ev'ry day on TV
   May provide an occasional thrill,
But the zaniest pair that you'll find on the air
   Are the gabby ones, Oprah and Phil.

It was Donahue first who came on with a burst,
   Though back then competition was nil;
Even so, it was clear from his very first year
   That great fortune was waiting for Phil.

Any day you might see a condemned maître d'
   Or a lost tribe of dwarfs from Brazil;
Soon acclaimed on both coasts as the lord of the hosts
   Was the afternoon wonder called Phil.

Through his drive to succeed, it was mainly agreed
   There was no one to rival his skill;
And yet someone came, Oprah Winfrey by name,
   With one aim, to do battle with Phil.

She could fill up a screen like no emcee you've seen,
   And her mouth very seldom was still;
Like a geyser she'd gush, turning hearts into mush,
   Which, of course, was distressing to Phil.

He was taken aback by her fearless attack,
   As if pierced by a porcupine's quill;
And his ratings did slip as they fought lip to lip
   In the Battle of Oprah and Phil.

Now it's war ev'ry day as they prattle away
   For the right to be king of the hill;
Almost anything goes on their loony-tune shows
   In the Battle of Oprah and Phil.

You will hear from MDs who are curing disease
   With an ancient Peruvian pill,
Or two brothers who sleep with a born-again sheep
   When you tune in to Oprah or Phil.

Hear a housewife who swears Satan lives 'neath her stairs;
   See a Jack now rebuilt as a Jill;
Meet a farmer who chants while he's tortured by ants;
   They're all yakking with Oprah or Phil.

Full of fury they fight, with their tongues at full might,
   Each one hoping the other to kill;
Let us pray both succeed; only then we'll be freed
   From the Battle of Oprah and Phil.

Schwarzenegger

By the shores of the Pacific,
In the town of glitz and hustle,
Strode the mighty Schwarzenegger,
Baring chest and flexing muscle;
Biceps twitched in perfect rhythm
Through his skill with isometrics,—
Feats that Letterman, on seeing,
Sought to use as Stupid Pet Tricks.

But the bulging Schwarzenegger
Set his sights on goals much higher,
As the lure of movie stardom
Pumped him up with great desire;
Soon he found himself in epics,
Slaying enemies like vermin,
Tearing dialogue to pieces
With his accent, Anglo-German.

Clenching jaw, he raged as "Conan,"
Who, upset by double-dealing,
Slaughters half the population
To express his depth of feeling;
Next "The Terminator" starred him
As a droid bent on aggression,
Killing victims for two hours
Without changing his expression.

As a soldier in "Commando,"
On whole armies he was feasting,
Shrugging off a hail of bullets
Like a flea-bite or a bee-sting;
Not Stallone in Panavision
Matched the fury of his scowling
When in "Predator" he thrilled us
In the art of disemboweling.

In a further quest for glory
As "The Running Man" he bore up,
Bringing down the rule of evil
While assorted foes he tore up;
See him punch out his oppressors,
Rip apart a villain's torso,
Bludgeon killers into meatloaf
Like Chuck Norris, only more so.

Yes, the massive Schwarzenegger,
Muscles rippling, tendons straining,
Now, through fame and sky-high grosses,
As a superstar is reigning;
Let the critics crucify him
When his lines he seems to louse up;
If it's brains that wins the Oscars,
It's the beef that fills the house up.

Zoo's Who

The Aardvark

Compared to lions, wolves and chimps,
The aardvark hardly rates a glimpse,
 And yet remains the darling of the media;
He surely has no claim to fame,
So why do we promote his name?
 He's listed first in our encyclopedia.

The Penguin

You'll find no penguin in the air;
 It's not among his talents;
Instead, he waddles here to there
 And strives to keep his balance;
He's certainly no Fred Astaire—
 For him that's only normal;
At least, when there's some swank affair
 You know he'll show up formal.

The Python

The python puts the squeeze on foes—
 An exercise that dooms them—
And then, when in their final throes,
 He quietly consumes them;
Right now he has but one request:
 That some kind soul will guide him
To find a method to digest
 The elephant inside him.

The Yak

The yak seems like a mammoth mop,
  A shaggy apparition;
He won't go near a barber shop
  And runs from the beautician;
We quake before his dreadful roar,
  But, no, he won't attack us;
He's much too busy looking for
  A young seductive yakess.

The Bat

Bats are creepy; bats are scary;
Bats do not seem sanitary;
Bats in gloomy caves keep cozy;
Bats remind us of Lugosi;
Bats have webby wings that fold up;
Bats from ceilings hang down rolled up;
Bats when flying undismayed are;
Bats are careful; bats use radar;
Bats at nighttime at their best are;
Bats by Batman unimpressed are.

The Opossum

  The possum's found
  Above the ground
In forest, wood and dale;
  A branch or limb
  Is home to him,
And thereby hangs a tail.

The Zebra

The zebra says with great delight
His stripes are black, his coat is white;
Tomorrow he will take it back
And say his stripes are white on black;
Small wonder that we've come to doubt
The double talk he's handing out;
In truth, he really is, of course,
A psychedelic mini-horse.

The Shrew

Unawed by gnus
Or caribous
Or elephants or camels,
All shrews are proud
To be endowed
As nature's smallest mammals.

Should shrews refuse
To stay in zoos,
It's wrong to hold them blamable,
For if you've read
What Shakespeare said,
You'll know they're rarely tamable.

The Skunk

Whenever there's
A skunk with airs,
We always seem to smell him;
The fault's not his;
The problem is
His best friend will not tell him.

The Crocodile

We know that cats like liver
And that roosters holler "Cockle-doo!"
But in a jungle river,
No one's sure just what a croc'll do.

It's said he's fond of creeping
To the places where small fishes nap,
And, as they lie there sleeping,
To consume them with a vicious snap.

He has no fav'rite dishes,
Daily catching what he can for lunch,
And should he lack for fishes,
He may even have a man for lunch.

So if by chance you wind up
In his jungle river, then you, sir,
May find that you've been lined up
For the crocodile's menu, sir.

The Amoeba

Most creatures live domestic lives
As fathers, mothers, husbands, wives;
Amoebas have no urge to mate;
They live alone, don't even date;
But solitude, though free of strife,
Can prove a rather humdrum life,
So when, in time, they tire of it,
They bid themselves goodbye—and split.

The Dolphin

Behold the ocean's gadabout—
  The frisky, friendly dolphin;
His head displays a smiling snout;
  His backside sports a tall fin;
Content to frolic in the sea,
  He's never fierce or warlike;
How happier our world would be
  If dolphins we were more like.

The Sports Pages

You Are Old, Henry Aaron

"You are old, Henry Aaron," the southpaw said,
  "You are no longer able to hit;
Your swing has no zip and your timing is dead;
  Don't you think at your age you should quit?"

"You are right," Henry Aaron replied to the youth,
  "That my great slugging days should be through;
To prove to us both that you utter the truth,
  Why not pitch me a slider or two?"

"You are old," said the southpaw, approaching the mound,
  "And extinct as the Olduvai Man;
With luck you will dribble the ball on the ground—
  If not that, you will certainly fan."

"You are right," Henry Aaron replied, "to recall
  That I dodder and turn into seed;
Perhaps I may catch just a piece of the ball,
  Which would be a great triumph indeed."

"You are old," said the southpaw, his pitch on the way,
  "Of your fate there can be not a doubt;
And yet you persist in this hopeless display
  When you know in your heart you are out."

"You are right," Henry Aaron replied. "To my ear
  There is truth in your every remark;
But my bat, I discover, is deaf and I fear
  It has hit the ball out of the park."

O TV! My TV!

O TV! My TV!
Our day has just begun
With "Fishing Tips" at 10 a.m. and tennis, noon to one;
And, in between, a hockey game on tape from Montreal,
And then the finals, from Duluth, of college volleyball.

O TV! My TV!
Your presence fills my day
With highlights of last season's game 'twixt Cleveland and
    Green Bay;
And, after that, a look in depth at Foreman's knock-out
    punch,
And then a break for local news while I prepare my lunch.

O TV! My TV!
I haven't left your side;
At 4 there is a possum hunt—Frank Gifford is our guide;
And then to Sweden to observe a Frisbee match at night,
Concluded by a rugby game—all via satellite.

O TV! My TV!
The night is drawing nigh;
And on your screen a bobsled team of dwarfs is racing by;
And while I bolt my supper down, you show at 8:15
A croquet match, then analyze the current bungee scene.

O TV! My TV!
Our day comes to an end;
'Tis 2 a.m., O faithful pal, O most devoted friend;
And as we part, your final words I never shall forget—
How fitting that Cosell should preach your late-night
    Sermonette.

The Sunday Golfer

Under a tree that's in the rough
   The Sunday golfer hunts;
His ball is buried in the grass,
   And finding it, he grunts:
"I'll give myself a better lie,
   But only just this once."

He tees the ball upon a twig,
   Then shouts a mighty "Fore!"
And swings his club, which moves the ball
   A solid foot or more;
"A practice shot," he mumbles,
   "Which does not affect my score."

He swings again and watches while
   The ball curves in a hook,
Then mutters as it disappears
   Into a muddy brook:
"It's clear the ball was poorly made;
   This shot I'll overlook."

At last he makes it to the green,
   To where his colleagues are,
Then dribbles in a two-foot putt
   And, lighting a cigar,
Says, "What a day I'm having—
   I just made my seventh par."

Doubleday

In Cooperstown did Doubleday
The game of baseball dedicate;
In pastures did the fielders play
With splintered bats and balls like clay
   And pie-tins for home plate.

The early game was quite a thrill,
Which made the local fans agree
That though the players might lack skill
And second base was on a hill,
    The sport was fun to see.

The game has changed from days of yore,
With sliders slicing past each bat,
With players hitting .204,
And fifteen innings with no score,
    And dreadful things like that.

In sterile domes the public sees
The game played on a sunless field,
With unforeseen calamities,
Like twisted legs and torn-up knees,
    From turf that doesn't yield.

Rich superstars now reign supreme,
Each season holding out for more;
Though once we held them in esteem,
They leap with greed from team to team
    As ticket prices soar.

The cheated fans, it's they who pay
As down the twisted path they're led,
Which makes me think if Doubleday
The grand old game could now survey,
    He'd take up golf instead.

Baseball Types

The Pitcher

Before the ball is plateward bound,
The Pitcher dawdles on the mound;
He wipes his brow, hikes up his pants,
Reties his shoes, adjusts his stance;
It's surely not his wish, you know,
To make the game so dull and slow;
The truth revealed, he has to stall
For time to doctor up the ball.

The Catcher

Behind ten pounds of pads and mask,
The Catcher has a thankless task;
While pitchers throw and batters swat,
He's in a state of constant squat,
Deflecting fast-balls with his ear
And taking foul-tips on the rear;
Yet, through it all, he'll still persist
Like any normal masochist.

The First Baseman

The man at First is just a hulk
Of beefy, burly, brawny bulk;
His only job, the graceless lout,
Is catching balls to put men out;

He isn't fast; he isn't quick;
But no one seems to care a lick;
For, after all, who thinks of style
When he hits balls a country mile?

The Second Baseman

In courage and raw guts supreme,
The Second Baseman leads the team;
As middleman for double plays,
He throws to First, then gulps and prays
That somehow he will save his skin
From spikes and runner crashing in;
Can he avoid this dreadful fate?
Just see him jump—tch, tch—too late!

The Shortstop

We marvel at the Shortstop's art:
Just see him swerve and lunge and dart!
Of course, to some, it makes no sense
Because the ball just cleared the fence;
But in the field the Shortstop knows
That he must put on fancy shows;
How else can he make you and me
Forget he's batting .203?

The Third Baseman

Although he's sprawled out in the dirt,
The man at Third has not been hurt;
He's simply goofed another try

To stab a grounder bounding by;
He now exudes, to our regret,
An air that reeks of grime and sweat;
His teammates give him space and hope
He'll shower soon—with lots of soap.

The Outfielders

The man in Center, Left or Right
Presents a most heroic sight;
At crack of bat, he eyes the ball
And races bravely for the wall;
He smacks the concrete with his leap
And crumples in a mangled heap;
Three runs are scoring—what a shame
To lose an exhibition game.

The Manager

With shoulders stooped and body bent,
The Manager's a mournful gent;
Although he's not a holy man,
He's learned to pray as best he can;
This afternoon he's forced to see
His club lose 17 to 3;
No wonder that he has one dream—
To manage the opposing team.

A Rhyming Guide to Pro Football

The Offensive Team

The Quarterback

Observe the big-shot Quarterback
Now screwing up his team's attack;
He should be using all his wits
To plan his play and stop the blitz;
But now he's such a business whiz,
His mind is on those bars of his;
I guess he's now too big a name
To care about a silly game.

The Running Back

The Running Back's a special breed
Of lightning starts and blazing speed;
He's twice as fast as you or me
And runs the hundred in 9.3;
His quickness holds the fans enthralled;
They roar each time his number's called;
He takes the ball and, running hard,
Streaks up the middle—for a yard.

The Fullback

Behold this pile, this fleshy heap
Of guards and tackles seven deep;
Beneath them all and gasping air
You'll find the fullback smiling there;
Why does he smile, this beefy clod,
His head contorted in the sod?
Because he's just found out that he
Is lying on the referee.

The Offensive Line

When quizzed, the football maven knows
The names of all the high-paid pros,
But naming the Offensive Line
His memory will rarely shine;
It's time we praised this faceless bunch
Who hold the fort and take the crunch;
Their names are er, ulp (*choke*), ahem . . .
Well, one day we'll come up with them.

The Wide Receiver

You'll see this shifty chap rely
On patterns like the "post" or "fly,"
The "down-and-out" and "button-hook"
And countless others in the book;
The one that he prefers by far
Is called the "criss-cross zig-zag star";
Complex and tricky as this sounds,
He'll catch the football—out of bounds.

The Place-Kicker

No broken bones or aching joints
Beset this man who kicks the points;
He doesn't know from training drills,
From exercise or diet pills;
He only knows each time he kicks
He'll take the very least of licks;
His blockers, smelling play-off dough,
Will guard him and his precious toe.

The Defensive Team

The Front Four

These ends and tackles take great pride
In keeping surgeons occupied;
They've mastered their defensive arts,
Which means destroying vital parts;
With knuckles taped, they punch and maul
The luckless chap who has the ball;
Right now they're sad and sick to death;
The back they've creamed can still draw breath.

The Linebacker

This crouching beast of grunts and growls
Commits the most disgusting fouls;
In truth, he merely vents his wrath
Like any Stone Age psychopath;
He's fed raw meat and coaches think
He may be Darwin's missing link;
He should be caged, not running loose;
Let's hope that he can't reproduce.

The Cornerback

This man must stick with streaking ends
As if they were his closest friends,
And keep his eye out for the ball
Which sometimes isn't passed at all;
For even though the ends range deep
They're often decoys for a sweep;
Next play he'll catch his breath and then
They'll fake the poor sap out again.

The Kick Return Specialist

This player seldom glorified
Seems bent on instant suicide;
He lives each game in constant fear
And wonders if he'll last the year;
The ball's kicked high; he waits there grim
As tons of flesh descend on him;
Once crushed, he lies there deathly still;
Thank goodness he's made out his will.

The Failures

The High-Priced Rookie

This player was an all-time great
At Southeast Arizona State;
The Chargers spied him, if you please,
And signed him for one hundred G's;
He played one game and tried to pass
And met the Raider line en masse;
This year his shrine they'll dedicate
At Southeast Arizona State.

The Bench-Warmer

Way back in '86 or so
This hulk was picked by Buffalo,
Who saw the nature of his play
And wisely dumped him on Green Bay,
Who threw him in a mid-year trade
The Vikings wish they'd never made;
How come each club picks up this clown?
He knows the broads in every town.

The Coaching Staff

The Head Coach

The Head Coach paces up and down,
His face contorted in a frown;
A nervous wreck who fears the worse,
He bows his head and breathes a curse,
Then shakes his fist and kicks the dirt
And rips the collar off his shirt;
If now it seems like he's upset,
Just wait—the game's not started yet.

The Assistant Coaches

Each member of this motley crew
Has his respective job to do;
One coaches fullbacks; one helps ends;
One checks to see whose breath offends;
But one of them, you may have guessed,
Is twice as vital as the rest;
When teams are switched, it's he who's here
To slap each player on the rear.

The Trainer

Whenever players lack the will
They ask the Trainer for a pill;
He's got a red one that will dull
The aching of a broken skull;
He's got another colored blue
For yellow fever and the flu;
Of course, the players will attest
They like those groovy green ones best.

The Team Physician

"Hoo boy! There goes another knee!"
The Team Physician shouts with glee;
He shouts because it means that he
Can try new kinds of surgery;
Small wonder that his work he digs,
With all those human guinea pigs;
He hasn't had so much to do
Since D-Day back in World War II.

The Front Office

The Team Owner

It may appear a bit extreme
To pay 10 million for a team;
The Owner, who's a well-heeled gent,
Does not begrudge a penny spent;
He didn't put the money down
To be a big-shot in his town;
He only had a single aim—
To get a seat to watch the game.

The General Manager

This man believes, with brazen crust,
That he has earned the players' trust;
The truth be known, he can't be beat
At playing both sides of the street;
Mid-season, when the going's hard,
He'll praise each back and hail each guard;
But six months hence, at contract time,
They're hopeless bums, not worth a dime.

The TV Crew

The Play-by-Play Announcer

This man, all faithful viewers know,
Was once a jock who made All-Pro;
A network grabbed him, to its shame,
To cash in on his former fame;
And now each week we hear his drone—
A boring, bumbling monotone;
But, still, he's not so bad, we've found—
That is, if you turn off the sound.

The Color Man

This year five million fans will squawk
About this man's obnoxious talk;
He's got a gift for nasty cracks
And second-guessing quarterbacks;
With flannel gums and voice of tin
He loves to throw his two cents in;
From what we hear, we've got to say
That two cents won't buy much today.

And Last and Least ...

The Referee

I think that I shall never see
A shy or modest referee;
Whenever there's a clipping call,
He struts off yardage with the ball,
Then prances out to face the stands
And makes grand motions with his hands;
I wonder what he's like to see
When working games *not* on TV.

Mother Goose Meets the Environment

Sing a Song of Spillage

Sing a song of spillage—
   A tanker's fouled the shore;
Four-and-twenty black birds—
   They were white before.

Humpty Dumpty

Humpty Dumpty sat on a wall;
Humpty Dumpty smoked a Pall Mall;
All of the doctors told Humpty that he
Must quit or he'd never live past 33.

Humpty Dumpty said, "I shall quit";
Humpty Dumpty smoked not a bit;
Humpty from smog is beginning to choke;
What the hell, Humpty—you might as well smoke!

Twinkle, Twinkle, Little Star

Twinkle, twinkle, little star,
How I wonder what you are?
Up above the world so high,
Like a diamond in the sky.

Well, I'll tell you, little star,
I can't tell you what you are;
With the smoke and haze and pall
I'm not sure you're there at all.

Four Little Tigers

Four little tigers
Sitting in a tree;
One became a lady's coat—
Now there's only three.

Three little tigers
'Neath a sky of blue;
One became a rich man's rug—
Now there's only two.

Two little tigers
Sleeping in the sun;
One a hunter's trophy made—
Now there's only one.

One little tiger
Waiting to be had;
Oops! He got the hunter first—
Aren't you kind of glad?

Solomon Grundy

Solomon Grundy
Breathed on Monday,
Wheezed on Tuesday,
Sneezed on Wednesday,
Coughed on Thursday,

Gasped on Friday,
Gagged on Saturday,
Heaved on Sunday,
And that was a *good* week for Solomon Grundy.

Little Bo-Peep

Little Bo-Peep
Has lost her sheep
    And thinks they may be roaming;
They haven't fled;
They've all dropped dead
    From nerve gas in Wyoming.

Murray Had a Smelting Plant

Murray had a smelting plant,
Which made the people frown;
For every time he poured out wastes
He turned the river brown.

The people came to Murray's plant
To show their opposition;
But Murray laughed right in their face
And tore up their petition.

The people took the case to court
And Murray heard the judge
Declare the plant must never more
Pour out its icky sludge.

The judge invoked an ancient law
From eighteen fifty-nine,
Which meant that Murray had to pay
A fifteen-dollar fine.

Should Murray not obey the law,
It's good to know that when
He's hauled back in he'll have to pay
That fifteen bucks again.

Wee Willie Winkie

Wee Willie Winkie
Guns up and down
On his souped-up Harley,
Waking up the town;
If you think that Willie
Makes a racket, Mister,
Wait till Willie's brother
Turns on his transistor.

Hickety, Pickety

Hickety, pickety, my black hen,
She lays eggs for gentlemen;
Of course, it's very good indeed
They don't know what goes in her feed.

Little Miss Muffet

Little Miss Muffet
Collapsed on her tuffet
From swordfish and died in a minute;
    Along came a spider
    Who knelt down beside her
And said, " 'Twas the mercury in it."

Little Jack Horner

Little Jack Horner
Got sick in his corner
    From salmon and thereupon fainted;
The spider inspected
The brand Jack selected
    And said, "Seems like *everything's* tainted."

Five Great Lakes

Five great lakes;
Five great lakes;
See what we've done!
See what we've done!
The fish are all dead 'cause pollution's rife;
You can cut through the scum with a carving knife;
Did you ever see such a blight in your life
As five great lakes?

Down the Chimney with Clement Clarke Moore

The Month Before Christmas

'Twas a month before Christmas, and all through the store
Each department was dripping with Yuletide decor;
The Muzak was blaring an out-of-tune carol
And fake snow was falling on "Ladies' Apparel."

I'd flown many miles from the North Pole this day
To check on reports which had caused me dismay;
I'd come to this store for but one special reason:
To see for myself what went on at this season.

I hid in a corner and in a short while
I saw the store president march down an aisle;
He shouted an order to "Turn the store tree on!"
And also the "NOEL" in blinding pink neon.

Up high, grandly hanging from twin gold supports,
Four hundred pink angels flew over "Men's Shorts";
And towering over the rear mezzanine—
A 90-foot Day-Glo "Nativity Scene."

The clock on the wall said two minutes to nine;
The floorwalkers proudly all stood in a line;
I watched while the president smelled their carnations
Then called out his final command—"Man Your Stations!"

When out on the street there arose such a roar!
It rang to the rafters and boomed through the store!
It sounded exactly like street-repair drilling—
Or maybe another big Mafia killing.

I looked to the doors, and there banging the glass
Was a clamoring, shrieking, hysterical mass,
And I felt from the tone of each scream and each curse
That the Spirit of Christmas had changed for the worse.

41

The clock it struck nine and the door opened wide
And that great human avalanche thundered inside;
More fearsome than Sherman attacking Atlanta
Came parents and kiddies with just one goal—"Santa!"

In front stormed the mothers, all brandishing handbags
As heavy and deadly as 20-pound sandbags;
With gusto they swung them, the better to smash ears
Of innocent floorwalkers, buyers and cashiers.

Egged on by their parents, the kids had one aim:
To get to this man who was using my name;
They mobbed him and mauled him, the better to plead
For the presents they sought in their hour of greed.

The president watched with a gleam in his eye
As he thought of the toys that the parents would buy;
Of all Christmas come-ons, this crowd would attest
That a visit to "Santa" was clearly the best.

It all was too much for my soul to condone
And I let out a most unprofessional moan;
The crowd turned around, and I'll say for their sake
That they knew in an instant I wasn't a fake.

"I've had it," I told them, "with fast-buck promoting,
With gimmicks and come-ons and businessmen gloating;
This garish display of commercialized greed
Is so very UN-Christmas, it makes my heart bleed!"

With that, I departed and, shouting a farewell,
Went barreling up an emergency stairwell;
On reaching the roof, to my sleigh I went forth
Where my reindeer were waiting to take me back north.

The crowd swarmed behind me to beg me to stay;
Before they could speak, I was off in my sleigh;
But I turned to exclaim as I flew from the mob—
"Happy Christmas to all—I'm resigning my job!"

The 1981 Night Before Christmas

'Twas the night before Christmas, and one thing was clear—
That old yuletide spirit no longer was here;
Inflation was rising; the crime rate was tripling;
The fuel bills were up, and our mortgage was crippling.

I opened a beer as I watched the TV,
Where Donny sang "O Holy Night" to Marie;
The kids were in bed, getting sleep like they should;
Or else they were stoned, which was almost as good.

While ma with her ball-point was making a fuss
'Bout folks we'd sent cards to who'd sent none to us;
"Those ingrates," she thundered, and pounded her fist;
"Next year you can bet they'll be crossed off our list!"

When out in the yard came a deafening blare;
'Twas our burglar alarm, and I hollered, "Who's there?"
I turned on the searchlight, which lit up the night,
And, armed with my handgun, beheld a strange sight.

Some red-suited clown with a white beard immense
Was caught in our eight-foot electrified fence;
He called out, "I'm Santa! I bring you no malice!"
Said I, "If you're Santa, I'm Telly Savalas!"

But, lo, as his presence grew clearer to me,
I saw in the glare that it just might be he!
I called off our doberman clawing his sleigh
And, frisking him twice, said, "I think he's okay."

I led him inside where he slumped in a chair,
And he poured out the following tale of despair;
"On Christmas eves past I was jolly and chuckling,
But now 'neath the pressures, I fear I am buckling.

You'll note I've arrived with no reindeer this year,
And without them, my sleigh is much harder to steer;
Although I would like to continue to use them,
The wildlife officials believe I abuse them.

To add to my problem, Ralph Nader dropped by
And told me my sleigh was unsafe in the sky;
I now must wear seatbelts, despite my objections,
And bring in the sleigh twice a year for inspections.

Last April my workers came forth with demands,
And I soon had a general strike on my hands;
I couldn't afford to pay unionized elves,
So the missus and I did the work by ourselves.

And then, later on, came additional trouble—
An avalanche left my fine workshop in rubble;
My Allstate insurance was worthless, because
They had shrewdly slipped in a 'no avalanche' clause.

A week after that came an I.R.S. audit;
The government claimed I was out to defraud it;
They finally nailed me for 65 grand,
Which I paid through the sale of my house and my land.

And yet I persist, though it gives me a scare
Flying blind through the blanket of smog in the air;
Not to mention the hunters who fill me with dread,
Taking shots at my sleigh as I pass overhead.

My torn-up red suit, and these bruises and swellings,
I got fighting muggers in multiple dwellings.
And if you should ask why I'm glowing tonight,
It's from flying too close to a nuclear site."

He rose from his chair and he heaved a great sigh,
And I couldn't help notice a tear in his eye;
"I've tried," he declared, "to reverse each defeat,
But I fear that today I've become obsolete."

He slumped out the door and returned to his sleigh,
And these last words he spoke as he went on his way;
"No longer can I do the job that's required;
If anyone asks, just say, 'Santa's retired.' "

St. Nicholas Meets the Population Explosion

'Twas the night before Christmas, and all through the gloom
Not a creature was stirring; there just wasn't room;
The stockings were hanging in numbers so great,
We feared that the walls would collapse from the weight.

The children like cattle were packed off to bed;
We took a quick count; there were three-hundred head;
Not to mention the grown-ups—those untallied dozens
Of uncles and inlaws and twice-removed cousins.

When outside the house there arose such a din!
I wanted to look but the mob held me in;
With pushing and shoving and cursing out loud,
In forty-five minutes I squeezed through the crowd.

Outside on the lawn I could see a fresh snow
Had covered the people asleep down below;
And up in the sky what should strangely appear
But an overweight sleigh pulled by countless reindeer.

They pulled and they tugged and they wheezed as they
    came,
And the red-suited driver called each one by name:
"Now, Dasher! Now, Dancer! Now, Prancer and Vixen!
On, Comet! On, Cupid! On, Donder and Blitzen!

Now, Melvin! Now, Marvin! Now, Albert and Jasper!
On, Sidney! On, Seymour! On, Harvey and Casper!
Now, Clifford! Now, Max"—but he stopped, far from
    through:
Our welcoming house-top was coming in view.

Direct to our house-top the reindeer then sped
With the sleigh full of toys and St. Nick at the head;
And then like an earthquake I heard on the roof
The clomping and pounding of each noisy hoof.

Before I could holler a warning of doom,
The whole aggregation fell into the room;
And under a mountain of plaster and brick
Mingled inlaws and reindeer and me and St. Nick.

He panted and sighed like a man who was weary;
His shoulders were stooped and his outlook was dreary:
"I'm way behind schedule," he said with a sigh,
"And I've been on the road since the first of July."

'Twas then that I noticed the great, monstrous sack,
Which he barely could hold on his poor, creaking back;
"Confound it!" he moaned, "though my bag's full of toys,
I'm engulfed by the birthrate of new girls and boys."

Then, filling the stockings, he shook his sad face,
"This job is a killer; I can't take the pace;
This cluttered old world is beyond my control;
There even are millions up at the North Pole.

Now I'm late!" he exclaimed, "and I really must hurry!
By now I should be over Joplin, Missouri!"
But he managed to sigh as he drove out of sight,
"Happy Christmas to all, and to all a goodnight!"

Refeathering "The Raven"

The Reagan

Once upon a cold November, back in '80, you'll remember,
Came to pass a great election, with a wondrous change in
    store;
By a landslide, one was winning, promising a new begin-
    ning;
Tall and proud, he stood there, grinning, like so many times
    before;
Who was he, this cool one, grinning, like so many times
    before?
          'Twas The Reagan, nothing more.

Once he was inaugurated, Reaganomics he created,
Promising a balanced budget, like we had in days of yore;
"Though," he said, "our debt is growing, and a bundle we
    are owing,
I'll cut taxes, 'cause I'm knowing this will save us bucks
    galore";
"Please explain," a newsman asked, "how this will save us
    bucks galore?"
          Quoth The Reagan, "Less is more."

Pushing for defense, he pleaded, brand-new missiles would
    be needed:
"That's the only way," he said, "to keep the country out of
    war";
"True," he said, "they're not required, and they're not meant
    to be fired;
In five years they'll be retired—still we must build hundreds
    more";
"Tell us why," a newsman asked, "we must be building
    hundreds more?"
          Quoth The Reagan, "Jobs galore."

Was he real or from a movie? "Make my day" sure sounded
    groovy,
Standing up to Congress or the rebels in El Salvador;
Flicks like "Rambo" he promoted (sev'ral times, it should be
    noted);
Once John Wayne he even quoted, when Kaddafi threatened
    war;
"Does this mean," a newsman asked, "we're heading to-
    ward a Mid-East war?"
            Quoth The Reagan, "Hit the shore."

During times he wasn't dozing, many plans he was propos-
    ing,
Dealing with the deficit, which he no longer could ignore;
"Cuts," he said, "I'm recommending, pending our ascend-
    ing spending,
With attending trends suspending, then extending as be-
    fore."
"Does this mean," a newsman asked, "a balanced budget
    like before?"
            Quoth The Reagan, "Nevermore."

The Jogger

Once upon a morning dreary, half awake and eyesight
    bleary,
While I fetched the "Daily Herald" lying there outside my
    door,
As I stood there, stretching, yawning, wond'ring what the
    day was spawning,
Came a figure through the dawning, fiercely running as to
    war;
"Who is this," I asked myself, "who runs as if he's off to war?
            Just a loony, nothing more."

I could see his Pro-Keds clearly, and his perspiration nearly
Soaked right through the cotton sweatshirt and the running
    shorts he wore;

Shorter breaths he now was taking, and from grunts that he
    was making,
I felt sure he must be aching from the labors of his chore;
"Does your body ache," I asked, "each time that you per-
    form this chore?"
               Quoth the Jogger, "Ev'ry pore."

Striding down the street, he ran there, trotting past each
    parked sedan there,
Till the air was filled with gasps that I had not heard here-
    tofore;
Soon I knew as he came closer, he was not a loony, no sir,
Or some early-rising grocer racing toward some distant
    store;
"You're a Jogger," I exclaimed, "and not some grocer with a
    store!"
               Quoth the Jogger, "To the core."

Round the block he now was veering, then quite soon was
    reappearing,
Battered, scarred and bleeding in a state most people would
    deplore;
Ev'ry garment he was wearing now was either ripped or
    tearing;
Furthermore, his legs were bearing signs of toothmarks by
    the score;
"What on earth," I asked, "has caused these signs of tooth-
    marks by the score?"
               Quoth the Jogger, "Dogs galore."

Suddenly, it started raining, and I thought he'd be complain-
    ing
Of conditions unforeseen that Mother Nature had in store;
Drenched with rain, he soon was dripping, and sometimes
    he lost his gripping
Causing him to wind up slipping on the pavement bruised
    and sore;
"Give it up," I pleaded, as he lay there gasping, bruised and
    sore;
               Quoth the Jogger, "Let it pour."

On and on, he did continue, straining ev'ry bone and sinew,
Round the block and back again until each passing was a
    bore;
"Hey," I asked him, "aren't you done now? Surely this can't
    be much fun now;
Fifteen miles or more you've run now since I've been here,
    keeping score:
Isn't that enough?" I uttered, as I stood there, keeping score;
            Quoth the Jogger, "Just one more."

Then it was that I did see there just how old he seemed to be
    there;
Ancient was his weathered face with wrinkles I could not
    ignore;
Years of running so insanely made him look much older,
    plainly,
Than his age, which I felt mainly must be fifty-five or more;
"What's your age?" I asked, expecting he'd say fifty-five or
    more;
            Quoth the Jogger, "Twenty-four."

Seasoned to Taste

(3 parody recipes)

Chop Suey Ogden Nash

1 *pound veal steak*	2 *cups bean sprouts*
2 *tablespoons shortening*	¼ *cup all-purpose flour*
2 *cups chopped onions*	2 *tablespoons water*
2 *cups chopped celery*	2 *tablespoons soy sauce*

1 *can mushrooms*

Many Chinese for their meals take
Veal steak,
Which they cut in small pieces in their sampan
And brown in a skillet, which Orientals call a lamb pan;
After adding the onions, celery, and mushroom juices,
And an appropriate line from Confucius,
They cook the concoction for half an hour, give or take a
    minute,
Then throw the sprouts and mushrooms and a thick mixture
    of the flour, water, and soy sauce in it;
They could, it is true, put a sauce that is blander in,
But that would not be Cantonese and certainly not Manda-
    rin;
So they cook it all over a high flame for five minutes, to be
    precise,
Then finally serve it over Chinese noodles or rice;
If you follow all of the above instructions carefully, you will
    have enough to serve a party of six;
As for me, I'll use a mix.

Carrot Loaf Carl Sandburg

Two cups of Mashed, Cooked Carrots,
One-Half Teaspoon of Salt, One-Fourth Teaspoon
of Pepper, and One-Fourth Cup of Cream,
Two Eggs,
Broken, Opened, Slightly Beaten,
Two Tablespoons of Sugar,
White, Granulated, Pourable.

They tell me to mix thoroughly all of the ingredients and I
believe them, for I know the ingredients will mix thoroughly.

And they tell me to place the ingredients in a greased casse-
role and set in a pot of hot water and I answer: Yes, why
not?

And they tell me to bake in a moderate oven at 350 degrees
until firm, for about 45 minutes, and my reply is: I shall
wind my watch.

And having done all of these things, I turn the loaf out on a
hot platter and surround with buttered peas and say:
This is what can be made from Two Cups of Mashed,
Cooked Carrots, One-Half Teaspoon of Salt, One-
Fourth Teaspoon of Pepper, One-Fourth Cup of Cream,
Two Eggs, Broken, Opened, Slightly Beaten, Two Table-
spoons of Sugar, White, Granulated, Pourable.

Meringue Glacé Cole Porter

8 egg whites	*1 teaspoon vanilla*
2 cups sugar	*Pinch of salt*

When you begin the meringue—
Oh, darling, be sure
the whites are well beaten;

Then pour in, my pet,
  the sugar to sweeten—
When you begin the meringue.

When you begin the meringue—
The salt goes in next,
  and then the vanilla;
The moon will look down
  on our Spanish villa—
When you begin the meringue.

Although, little fool,
Two hearts may be aching,
You've got to hold on
  while stars burn above—
Just *whip it well*
  till a firm shape it's taking;
This dish that you're making
  is our love.

When you begin the meringue—
You must spoon it out in small *rings*
  and bake at 250;
A mere 30 minutes is *nice*—
  it's neater than nifty;
When you begin the meringue.

So, *dar-ling*—
Won't you begin the meringue—*start today!*
And with ice cream spread on top,
  the gods will guide us—
There is such a hungry yearning
  burning inside us!
And all through the night,
We'll conquer the pang—
When you begin the meringue.

The Immortal Casey

Casey at the Talks

It looked extremely rocky for the famous Mudville nine;
The season was upon them and the outfield wouldn't sign;
And when Fenwick turned free agent and Moran went into
    flicks,
The owners shook their heads and moaned, "We're in a
    dreadful fix."

They scanned their ledgers gloomily without a hint of cheer;
The falling season-ticket sales foretold a losing year;
They clung to one small, distant hope, an optimistic dream—
The fans would pack the stands with mighty Casey on the
    team.

For Casey was a superstar that any club would prize,
Who last year led the league in hits, home runs and RBIs;
For months the phone-calls made to him were scornfully
    declined;
A god he was, unreachable and, what was worse, unsigned.

Then from an outer corridor there rose a mighty shout;
It rattled the reception desk and shook the walls throughout;
It thundered through the offices in one tremendous roar,
For Casey, mighty Casey, was advancing through the door.

There was pride in Casey's manner, there was class in
    Casey's style,
As he touched each owner's hand and gave a patronizing
    smile;
He'd brought with him six solemn men, their faces grim and
    grave—
Two lawyers, three accountants and his business agent,
    Dave.

The owners lauded Casey's clothes, extolled his wavy hair;
They kissed the leather of his shoes and knelt beside his
      chair;
They laid before him fruit and wine and then a full-course
      meal,
But Casey merely raised his hand and murmured, "What's
      your deal?"

"Five million bucks is yours," they said, "for playing out the
      year,
Plus 10 percent of grandstand sales of ballpark franks and
      beer;
When on the road we'll line up broads, of whom you'll have
      your choice,
Plus shares of stock, a butler and a custom-built Rolls-
      Royce."

The smile is gone from Casey's lips, his countenance is stern;
He grips his chair with knuckles white, he gives his head a
      turn;
And now he flicks an eyebrow at his agent standing by,
And now the air is shattered by the words of his reply.

Oh, somewhere in the baseball world there is a happy town,
Where management has signed a star who'll win the triple
      crown;
And somewhere fans stand up to cheer a bases-loaded clout,
But there is no joy in Mudville—mighty Casey has held
      out.

Casey at the Dice

The table wasn't breaking for the Vegas crowd that night;
The house was up 12 big ones with no change of luck in sight.
So, when Epstein came out snake-eyes, and Spinelli missed
      his point,
A mood of deep depression could be felt throughout the
      joint.

The dollar-bettors, cleaned of cash, were heading out the
    door,
But all the big high-rollers stayed to even up the score;
They said: "If only Casey had a chance to roll the dice,
We'd have a shot to change our luck, which now is cold as
    ice!"

Then, suddenly, their eyes lit up; a cry rose from their lips;
It echoed off the slot machines, it rattled off the chips;
It rumbled through the blackjack games while cards were
    being dealt;
For Casey, lucky Casey, was advancing to the felt!

His nails were cleanly manicured, his face was richly tanned,
His suit was iridescent silk that cost him half a grand;
The cuff-links on his sheer batiste were rubies from afar;
Between his teeth he coolly smoked a ninety-cent cigar.

There was ease in Casey's manner as he calmly placed his
    bet;
His hands were steady as a rock, his palms were free of
    sweat;
The other shooters, now revived, together had one goal:
To place each C-note they had left on Casey and his roll.

With confidence he gripped the cubes, his bearing cool and
    calm,
Then blowing on them softly, let them nestle in his palm.
"A seven, dice," he murmured, as he looked up to the sky,
And a hush went 'round the table as he raised his arm on
    high.

The cool is drained from Casey's face, his eyes are tense and
    keen;
And all along his sun-drenched brow deep furrows can be
    seen;
And now he firmly holds the dice, and now he lets them go,
And now the air is shattered by the force of Casey's throw!

Oh, somewhere in this wealthy land there is a happy spot
Where naturals are being rolled and dice are running hot;
And somewhere men are doubling up and winners scream
    and shout;
But there is no joy in Vegas—lucky Casey has crapped out.

The Poetry Round-Robin Roundelay

If Poe's "The Raven" Were Written by Joyce Kilmer

I think that I shall never hear
A raven who is more sincere
Than that one tapping at my door
Who's ever saying, "Nevermore";
A raven who repeats his words
Until I think I'm for the birds;
A raven who, I must assume,
Will dirty up my living-room;
A raven fond of bugs and worms
With whom I'm on the best of terms;
Let other poets praise a tree—
A raven's good enough for me.

If Kilmer's "Trees" Were Written by John Masefield

I must go up in a tree again, from where people look like
    ants,
And all I ask is a branch that's smooth so I won't rip my
    pants;
And a dozen bugs running up my leg, and the sap so sticky,
And the cooing doves and the screaming crows making
    messes icky;

I must go up in a tree again and sit where the bullfinch
    warbles;
Where the squirrel runs up and down a limb and the owl has
    lost his marbles;
And the squawks and hoots and chirps and squeaks that all
    the birds are making
Fill the air around so I can't hear the branch beneath me
    breaking.

If Masefield's "Sea Fever" Were Written by Carl Sandburg

Fish Tank for the World,
Shark Breeder, Maker of Waves,
Lousy with Herring and the Nation's Saltcellar;
Briny, bottomless, undrinkable,
Home of the Big Flounder:
They tell me you are stormy, and I believe them; for I have
    crossed you on a tramp steamer and have lost my lunch
    at the poop rail.
And they tell me you are messy, and my reply is: Yes, it
    is true I have swum in your surf and have emerged
    yecchy, with seaweed.
And having answered, I ask myself: Why am I not writing a
    poem about Chicago instead of a poem about the Fish
    Tank for the World, Shark Breeder, Maker of Waves,
    Home of the Big Flounder, and Saltcellar to the Nation?

If Sandburg's "Chicago" Were Written by Rudyard Kipling

You can talk of Mandalay,
Of Calcutta or Bombay,
    Where the heat'll make a fuzzy-wuzzy fry;

But if to drink you're driven
And don't give a damn for livin'
   Then you oughta hit the road for windy Chi.

It's a town where hoods and thugs
Like to send a dozen slugs
   Right through a copper pretty as you please;
Where the breezes blow like hell,
And that awful stockyard smell
   Is enough to bring a blighter to his knees.

For it's Chi! Chi! Chi!
Guns are shootin' and I'm just a passerby!
Though your buildings may be pretty,
You can keep your bloomin' city
'Cause I'm headin' back to Injia, windy Chi!

If Kipling's "Gunga Din" Were Written by Clement Clarke Moore

'Twas the night of the battle, and all through the slaughter,
Not a creature was stirring—we all needed water;
The canteens were slung on the sand-dunes with care,
In hopes that old Gunga Din soon would be there;
When what should appear to our wondering eyes
But a skinny brown native—oh, what a surprise!
I cheered with delight as he crossed a ravine,
For I knew right away that it was Gunga Din!
His garment was merely a cute little rag,
And he brought along with him a big water bag.
Then he went right to work in a manner quite shocking—
He shunned our canteens and instead filled each stocking!
It all seemed so senseless and, making things worse,
I knew there was something quite wrong with this verse.
I remarked, "What a strange thing to do in a war!"
And he said, "That's because you are Clement Clarke
      Moore;
I'm confused by your verses, so rhythmic and rippling—
Please write about Christmas, and give me back Kipling!"

If Moore's "A Visit from St. Nicholas" Were Written by Robert W. Service

A bunch of the boys were whooping it up on a Christmas
  Eve one year,
All full of cheap whiskey and hoping like hell that St. Nick
  would soon appear,
When right through the door and straight out of the night,
  which was icy and cold as a freezer,
Came a broken-down sled, pulled by eight mangy dogs,
  which were whipped by an old bearded geezer.

His teeth were half missing, and flapping his frame was a
  tatter of red-colored clothes;
He was covered with snow from his head to his toe, and an
  icicle hung from his nose;
The miners all cheered when the geezer appeared, and the
  poker game stopped in mid-bet;
Each sourdough smiled like a young, happy child at the
  thought of the gifts he would get.

They pushed him aside and went straight for his bag to be
  sure that they'd all get their share;
And, oh, how they cried when they found that inside there
  was nothing but old underwear;
So they plugged the old geezer, which was a great shame, for
  if anyone there had been sober,
He'd have known double-quick that it wasn't St. Nick,
  'cause it only was early October.

If Service's "The Shooting of Dan McGrew" Were Written by Henry Wadsworth Longfellow

Listen, my children, and I'll tell you
Of the valiant death of Dan McGrew;
With a patriot's pride he made his stand
While foes assailed his native land
And threatened to tear down the red, white and blue.

When the struggle for freedom lay hanging in doubt,
He cried to the bartender, with a fierce shout—
"One if it's whiskey, and two if it's beer!"
He drank like a man who had nothing to fear,
While brave men around him were all passing out.

At last, the dread enemy came into view,
And a cowardly bullet cut down Dan McGrew;
How the hopes of a nation were shattered that night!
And yet men could say as they took up the fight—
"A bullet achieved what no rotgut could do!"

If Longfellow's "The Midnight Ride of Paul Revere" Were Written by Ernest Lawrence Thayer

It looked extremely rocky for the Colonists that night;
The British were attacking with no hope of help in sight;
So, with villages in danger from the enemy so near,
They had to send a warning, and they called on Paul Revere.

There was ease in Paul's demeanor as he climbed upon his
    mare;
There was pride in Paul's expression as he sat so tall and fair;
And then the horse grew skittish, and she gave a sudden
    jump,
And Paul fell from his saddle, landing smack upon his rump.

With a smile of Yankee courage, Paul rose smartly to his feet,
And once again upon the saddled mare he took his seat;
But as he gripped the reins, she made a sudden turn around,
And once again Paul plummeted onto the dusty ground.

The smile has vanished from Paul's face, his eyes burn with a
    glare;
He grips the bridle fiercely as again he mounts the mare;
And now he tells the horse to gallop, in an urgent tone,
And now the air is shattered as the horse takes off—alone.

Oh, somewhere in this war-torn land the people safely know
That Redcoats are invading, taking captives as they go;
And somewhere people are prepared to flee the British force,
But there's no hope for New England—Paul Revere can't
    ride a horse.

If Thayer's "Casey at the Bat" Were Written by Edgar Allan Poe

Once upon a final inning, with the other ball-team winning,
And my Mudville teammates trailing by a score of 2 to 4,
With two outs, my fate it beckoned, for with men on third
    and second,
I could win the game, I reckoned, or at least tie up the score;
Crazed, I was, that final inning, just to win or tie the score—
    Only that, and nothing more.

Ghastly, gaunt and grim I stood there, gripping my great bat
    of wood there;
In my brain dark, ugly demons danced a dirge from days of
    yore;
Then the fast-ball came by flying, and, inside, my soul was
    dying
As I heard the umpire crying words from baseball's ancient
    lore:

"Strike one!" were the words he hollered, out of baseball's
    ancient lore—
            Just "Strike one!" and nothing more.

Once again I stood there quaking, while a curve-ball
    whizzed by, breaking;
How I wished that awful aching in my soul I could ignore!
But, alas, my fear grew colder, and the bat stayed on my
    shoulder,
While the ump, his voice now bolder, called out "Strike
    two!" with a roar;
Wretched was the dread within me as I heard his awful
    roar—
            Just "Strike two!" and nothing more.

Praying for some god to guide me, hope, I feared, would be
    denied me
While the tell-tale heart inside me beat upon some distant
    shore;
Then the change-up came by, looming, and I swung, my fate
    now dooming,
While the umpire's call came booming, and it chilled me to
    the core;
Ghostly was the call he thundered, chilling me right to the
    core—
            Just "Strike three!" and nothing more.

Mother Goose Around the World

In Japan . . . Sing a Song of Sonys

Sing a song of Sonys—
A pocketful of yen;
RCA and Zenith
Undersold again;
See the U.S. suffer
From the job we do;
This is how we get revenge
For losing World War II.

In the Middle East . . . Solomon Grundy

Solomon Grundy
Arrived here on Monday,
Ducked bullets on Tuesday,
Took cover on Wednesday,
Was blasted on Thursday,
Assaulted on Friday,
Bombarded on Saturday,
Ambushed on Sunday;
So much for the peacekeeping mission of Solomon Grundy.

In Central America . . . Taffy Was a Strongman

Taffy was a strongman;
Taffy used his clout;
Taffy led an armed revolt
    And drove his rival out;
Taffy bled the country;
Taffy made a haul;
Taffy lasted 14 days,
    Which isn't bad at all.

In Russia . . . The Old Woman in the Shoe

There was an old woman who lived in a shoe
With Boris, ten kids and a pet kangaroo;
She said, "Though it's cramped and from feet it is smelling,
In Moscow, it's known as a luxury dwelling."

In France . . . Mary Had a Small Café

Mary had a small café;
The meals she served were nice;
And ev'ryone who came agreed
She charged a modest price.

Mary's prices now are high;
How come? Well, here's the reason—
Today officially begins
A brand-new tourist season.

In Saudi Arabia . . . Humpty Dumpty

Humpty Dumpty drilled a new well;
Humpty Dumpty leased it to Shell;
He's now worth a billion, this fortunate gent,
And entertains friends in his 20-room tent.

Humpty Dumpty lives like a king;
Humpty Dumpty knows a good thing;
And that's why each day he is thanking his stars
For people still driving those gas-guzzling cars.

In Italy . . . Little Miss Muffet

Little Miss Muffet
   Got up from her tuffet
And made a big pot of linguine,
   With baked macaroni
   And sliced provolone,
Lasagna and veal scallopine.

Little Miss Muffet
   Plopped down on her tuffet,
Digesting the food that went in her;
   She burped, then confided,
   "I'm glad I decided
To have a small snack before dinner."

In Colombia . . . Peter, Peter

Peter, Peter, coffee grower,
Found his business getting slower;
Looked to make a greater gain,
Now makes a bundle from cocaine.

Peter, Peter, big supplier,
Sees his profits rising higher;
"Drugs are where it's at," he says;
"For coffee, go see Juan Valdez."

Poets for Hire

Henry Wadsworth Longfellow as a Used Car Dealer

Under the sign that says "Great Buy!"
  The Buick Regal stands;
Two thousand dollars is the price
  This gorgeous car commands
(In truth, I'd take one-fourth of that
  To get it off my hands).

I drove it and the ride was smooth
  (Except for when it stalled);
The engine's good for many years
  (If it were overhauled);
It's like you're in a car that's new
  (And should have been recalled).

It costs a small amount to run
  (If you can get free gas);
It's peppy and has speed to spare
  (Unless you want to pass);
On roads, it handles like a dream
  (If you've been smoking grass).

The seats will give you room to spare
  (And also ailments spinal);
You'll like the ultra-leather look
  (Another term for vinyl);
So drive this beauty home today
  (Bring cash; all sales are final).

Walt Whitman as a Mafia Don

O Capo! My Capo!
Our future is in doubt;
A rival gang is moving in and hopes to squeeze us out;
Last week, I fear, while on a job, Tartini took three slugs;
I grieve, old friend, that we may lose our chief supply for
    drugs.

O Capo! My Capo!
I feel alone and lost;
A rat is here within our midst; I'm being double-crossed;
Great sadness fills my aching heart to do what I must do,
Because I've found, dear friend of old, the rat, alas, is you.

John Masefield as a Pro Football Linebacker

I must go out on the field again and play for the Green Bay
    Pack;
And all I ask is a taped-up fist and a quarterback I can sack;
And a head to twist, and some knees to bust, and a half-
    crazed coach to lead me;
And some ribs to crack, and the grunts I make from the raw
    meat that they feed me.

I must go out on the field again and play for my old team;
Where I can hear the wondrous sound of a gang-tackled
    runner's scream;
And a nose to break, and an eye to gouge, and cleats to
    stomp a toe with;
And the body's thud, and the smell of blood, and the stats to
    make All-Pro with.

Robert W. Service as a TV Weatherman

A mass of cool air is churning it up down the whole Atlantic
    coast,
And out in the West it's so dog-dirty hot that it's making a
    rattlesnake roast;
In Ohio some snow is beginning to blow and they're due for
    a blizzard or two;
And up in the skies, folks are peeling their eyes for the
    Hurricane known as Sue.

In north Idaho nights are 50 below from a cold front up
    Canada way;
And that low-pressure mass that had started to pass just
    keeps hanging around day to day;
They're choking from dust from a high-pressure gust that
    keeps blowing from Texas right through;
And from here to Moline folks are looking real keen for that
    Hurricane known as Sue.

They're flooded from rains on the Great Western Plains, and
    from Michigan on to the East
They're starting to freeze from a cold, icy breeze that ain't fit
    for a man or a beast;
You might wonder, I guess, from this weatherman's mess, if
    the forecast's for rain or for shine—
If everything fails, flip a coin heads or tails, 'cause your guess
    is no better than mine.

Edgar Allan Poe as a Pharmacist

See my bottles full of pills—
    Pretty pills!
Packed with potent powder for the curing of your ills!
    I've a dandy bunch of new ones
      Good for snakebite or the grippe;
    And I've also got a few ones—

Some are yellow, some are blue ones—
     That will end your nasal drip;
  For I know, know, know,
  You'll pay half a buck a throw
To relieve irregularity, or muscle aches or chills
     With the pills, pills, pills, pills,
          Pills, pills, pills—
With your never-ending gulping of the pills.

        See my other kinds of pills—
             Happy pills!
Crammed with crazy chemicals that give all kinds of thrills!
     When my purple ones you're trying,
          There's a tingle that you feel;
     With the green ones, you'll be flying
     Till you're soon identifying
          With some world that isn't real;
     Feel that glow, glow, glow,
     Till your mind begins to blow
And you're hooked until you're swallowing that overdose
     that kills
          From the pills, pills, pills, pills,
               Pills, pills, pills—
From your never-stopping popping of the pills.

Carl Sandburg as a Travel Writer

LAS VEGAS

Crap Table for the World,
Card Dealer, Stacker of Chips,
Graveyard of Suckers and the Nation's Debt Maker,
Greedy, Grabby, Unbeatable City of the Lost Bankroll:
They tell me you are heartless, and I believe them; for I have
     seen the tourist from Omaha lose his rent money and
     then return with a cash advance on his Visa Card and
     lose again.

And they tell me you are treacherous, and I answer: Yes, I
    have seen the blackjack dealer hit a sixteen and make a
    twenty-one when I am holding a natural twenty.
And they tell me you are brutal, and my reply is: On the faces
    of high-rollers, I have seen the anguish of crapping out
    to the tune of five big ones.
And having answered, so I turn once more to those who run
    this city, and I say to them: Better I should spend a week
    in Philadelphia bored out of my skull than try to beat the
    Crap Table of the World, Card Dealer, Stacker of Chips,
    Graveyard of Suckers and City of the Lost Bankroll.

Rudyard Kipling as a Job Consultant

If you can get yourself a fancy title,
    Though no one knows just what your job's about;
If you can screw up projects that are vital,
    Then shift the blame before they find you out;
If you can treat a rival like a brother,
    Then stab him in the back each chance you can;
If you can steal the program of another,
    Then take the credit that it was your plan;

If you can rig expenses that are phony,
    While ev'ryone believes that they are real;
If you can take long lunches with a crony,
    And make your boss believe you've closed a deal;
If you can get the office staff to love you,
    When in your heart of hearts you think they're dirt;
If you can look alive to those above you,
    When nine to five no effort you exert;

If you can seem free-thinking and courageous,
    Yet always end up siding with your boss;
If you can get a mammoth raise in wages,
    Yet make him feel you're working at a loss;
If ev'ry line that's written here you've noted,
    And ev'ry rule and precept you obey,
Then to the highest spot you'll be promoted,
    Unless, of course, you're knifed along the way.

Keep the Meter Running

The Wondrous Woodstock Fair

I remember, I remember,
The wondrous Woodstock Fair;
In August, '69, it was,
And all the Heads were there;
Four hundred thousand made the trip,
So Walter Cronkite says,
To groove the Who, the Grateful Dead,
Canned Heat, and Joan Baez.

I remember, I remember,
The traffic unforeseen
That clogged the lanes for countless miles
On Highway 17;
And even while I write this verse
I fear there is no doubt
That many drivers still are there
Attempting to get out.

I remember, I remember,
That bleary, bombed-out mass
That wandered 'round the countryside
Freaked out on hash and grass;
Not all of them, I wish to say,
Possessed a glassy stare;
A few, in fact, could still recall
The reason they were there.

I remember, I remember,
That groovy, swinging scene,
That field of wheat that soon became
An open-air latrine;
And how it warmed our happy hearts
And filled us with good cheer
To know the farmer wouldn't need
To buy manure next year.

I remember, I remember,
That cataclysmic flood
Of rain that tumbled from the sky
And turned the Fair to mud;
And how the crowd threw off its clothes
And mingled in the bare,
Until the place looked something like
The final scene of "Hair."

I remember, I remember,
The way my nights were spent—
The pleasure when I bedded down
Inside my little tent;
And how I found, on waking up,
That all men were my brothers;
That I'd been joined throughout the night
By forty-seven others.

I remember, I remember,
The wondrous Woodstock Fair;
But wait—I haven't told you of
The rock that I heard there;
I'd really like to fill you in,
But much to my dismay,
The closest that I got to it
Was seven miles away.

The Village Hippie

Under his pad on 10th and B
  The Village Hippie stands;
A turned-on acid-head is he
  With pale and shaking hands;
And the flower jacket that he wears
  Hangs down in tattered strands.

His hair is long and blonde and curled;
    He sets it when he can;
His face is caked with unwashed grime
    That looks just like a tan;
And when he's near, you sort of wish
    He'd use Right Guard or Ban.

His pad is but a place for him
    To freak out in a crash;
The mouldy mattress on the floor
    Contains his secret stash—
In case the Narcs come busting in
    To glom his pot and hash.

His roomies, high on boo and coke,
    Are fogged in smoky swirls;
And as the Hippie tunes in on
    Their dungarees and curls,
He thinks it might be possible
    That some of them are girls.

No hang-ups bug his spaced-out world;
    He has no pressing need;
Last night he flew on LSD;
    Tonight he'll cop a weed;
Tomorrow he'll flip out of sight
    And blow his mind on speed.

The years fly by, and now let's see
    The Hippie we once knew;
His hair's turned white; his teeth are gone;
    His mind is rotted through;
Who ever thought he'd live to reach
    The age of thirty-two?

The Saga of AT&T

It was many and many a year ago,
    In the land of the brave and the free,
That a firm did arise and soon grew to great size,
    And its name was AT&T;
But its foes cried, "Unfair! You can't hog the whole share!
    A monopoly's bad as can be!"
And they fought very tough and in time, sure enough,
    They were breaking up AT&T.

Thus began a great war like no battle before,
    With a dozen firms running amok;
On came Sprint, MCI, sev'ral more shooting high
    For a slice of the long-distance buck;
And they snow you with ads pushing trendy, new fads,
    Like no hustle you ever did see;
Till you fall for their pitch and you're making the switch,
    Waving bye-bye to AT&T.

Soon you're making a call to a guy in St. Paul,
    When you're hearing a horrible screech;
So you ring him once more and are reaching a store
    Selling kitchen supplies in Palm Beach;
So you're trying again and are getting through when
    You discover your line has gone dead;
And you're fit to be tied, which is when you decide
    That you'll write him a letter instead.

Once a month you get ill from a 14-page bill
    Full of charges you can't comprehend,
Plus a plan ultra-new, bringing savings to you
    Just so long as more money you spend;
Everywhere that you look, there's more gobbledygook
    As they tout Fiber Optics and such,
And you're cursing your luck and you feel like a schmuck
    While your dollars they reach out and clutch.

Yes, they're making a haul when a Talk Line you call,
    And you're ripped off at two bucks a pop;
Check the bundle you've blown for that self-destruct phone
    You bought "cheap" in some ding-a-ling shop;

See that pile on the floor full of phone-books galore
    That not even a pack rat would save;
When you're done, put your ear to the ground and you'll
        hear
    Mister Bell turning 'round in his grave.

Now we're told all the time, it's a terrible crime
    When some giant monopoly rules;
"Competition's the way," the economists say,
    Which is what we are taught in our schools;
But from seeing the mess screwing up the U.S.,
    Any imbecile plainly can see
Life was better back then in those ancient days when
    We were screwed just by AT&T.

Fame

Alfred Adler, analysing,
    Probed the psyche, saw obsessions;
Bela Bartok, improvising,
    Blended chords in odd progressions;
Calvin Coolidge, silent, solemn,
    Thought of running, didn't choose to;
Dorothy Dix inscribed a column,
    Lulled the lovelorn, made them news, too;
Edward Elgar, mad for marches,
    Wrote five *Pomp and Circumstances*;
Fannie Farmer knew her starches,
    Turned out cookbooks, saved romances;
Greta Garbo, hibernating,
    Fled from films with little laughter;
Henry Hudson, navigating,
    Edged the Arctic, died soon after;
Ilya Ilf, pooh-poohing purges,
    Razzed Red Russians with wry stories;
Jesse James, obeying urges,
    Stole from banks, gained outlaw glories;

Kublai Khan found home-life dreary,
  Conquered Asia, met the Polos;
Lotte Lehmann sang *Valkyrie,*
  Filled up halls for *lieder* solos;
Margaret Mitchell, done with Scarlett,
  Wrote no more, abandoned Tara;
Nita Naldi, sultry starlet,
  Played the siren, echoed Bara;
Oliver Optic fed the hopper,
  Dashed off books for fledgling readers;
Pontius Pilate came a cropper,
  Proved the least of lesser leaders;
Quisling, quisling, tried for treason,
  Lost his life with few men grieving;
Robert Ripley, straining reason,
  Dug up facts beyond believing;
Sarah Siddons lit up stages,
  Woke the critics from their slumbers;
Thomas Telford earned his wages,
  Threw up bridges in great numbers;
Ugolino, unaesthetic,
  Sold out Pisa, drew damnation;
Vladimir Vasek waxed poetic,
  Mourned in metre Czech privation;
William Wallace sought no respite,
  Rallied clans, was hanged in London;
Xerxes, xenophobic despot,
  Lost a navy, wound up undone;
Yen Yang-chu attained his wishes,
  Streamlined Chinese ways of learning;
Zoltan Zandar, quite fictitious,
  Ends this piece, his fame thus earning.